WILD ABOUT SNAKES

RATTLESNAKES

BY HEATHER L. MONTGOMERY

Consultant:
Robert Mason, PhD
Professor of Zoology
J.C. Braly Curator of Vertebrates
Oregon State University, Corvallis

CAPSTONE PRESS
a capstone imprint

Edge Books are published by Capstone Press,
151 Good Counsel Drive, P.O. Box 669, Mankato, Minnesota 56002.
www.capstonepub.com

Library of Congress Cataloging-in-Publication Data
Montgomery, Heather L.
  Rattlesnakes / by Heather Montgomery.
  p. cm. — (Edge books. Wild about snakes)
  Includes bibliographical references and index.
  Summary: "Describes rattlesnakes including their distinctive
characteristics, habitats, and defenses"—Provided by publisher.
  ISBN 978-1-4296-5434-0 (library binding)
  ISBN 978-1-4296-6258-1 (paperback)
  1. Rattlesnakes—Juvenile literature. I. Title. II. Series.
QL666.O69M659 2011
597.96'38—dc22   2010025209

Editorial Credits
Kathryn Clay and Anthony Wacholtz, editors; Kyle Grenz, designer; Eric Gohl,
  media researcher; Eric Manske, production specialist

Photo Credits
Alamy/A & J Visage, 23 (right); John Cancalosi, 27; Universal Images Group
  Limited, 12 (left)
Getty Images Inc./David McNew, 22–23; Flickr/Marc Crumpler, 25; National
  Geographic/Bianca Lavies, 21, 28; National Geographic/Joel Sartore, 5;
  Visuals Unlimited/Joe McDonald, 15
Newscom, 8–9
Shutterstock/Amee Cross, 1; Andys, 12–13; Audrey Snider-Bell, cover, 14;
  Darren Green, 20; malko, 9 (person silhouette); Marilyn Volan, background;
  markrhiggins, 6; Paunovic, 9 (snake silhouette); Rusty Dodson, 10; Stephen
  Mcsweeny, 16–17; visuelldesign, 19

Printed in the United States of America in Stevens Point, Wisconsin.
092010   005934WZS11

TABLE OF CONTENTS

Chapter 1

A FINELY TUNED MACHINE

You freeze with one foot in the air over what looks like a pile of dead leaves. A rattling sound has stopped you mid-step. The leaf pile is actually a coiled mass of muscle—it's a rattlesnake! Good thing the rattlesnake warned you it was there.

If you find a snake with a triangular head, slit-like pupils, and camouflage colors, it may be a rattlesnake. If it has a rattle, you know for sure. Rattlers are the only snakes on the planet with rattles on their tails.

The rattle is just one of the many body parts that make rattlesnakes unique. Rattlesnakes also have special fangs and the ability to hunt in total darkness. Because these **reptiles** are so well equipped, their bodies work like finely tuned machines.

reptile—a cold-blooded animal that breathes air and has a backbone; most reptiles lay eggs and have scaly skin

Today about 30 different **species** of rattlesnakes live in North, Central, and South America. Rattlers usually live in dry areas like deserts. But they can also survive in thick forests, soggy swamps, and rocky mountain ranges.

Some rattlesnakes, such as the eastern massasauga rattlesnake and the western rattlesnake, can live as far north as Canada. When the weather is cool, they may only come out in the warmth of the day. They spend the rest of their time underground.

In the United States, rattlesnakes can be found in every state except Alaska, Hawaii, and Maine. Arizona has more species of rattlers than any other state.

Rattlesnake Range

☐ where rattlesnakes live

North America

Europe

Asia

Africa

South America

Australia

Antarctica

N
W ← E
S

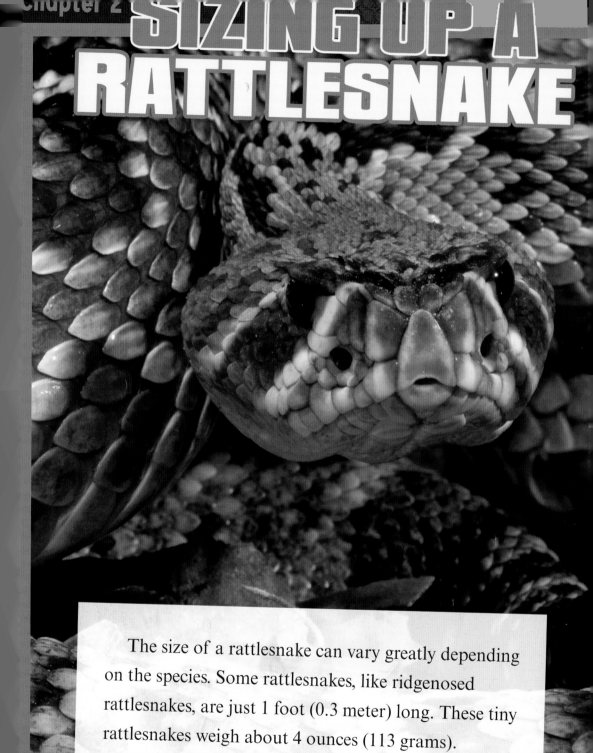

Chapter 2

SIZING UP A RATTLESNAKE

The size of a rattlesnake can vary greatly depending on the species. Some rattlesnakes, like ridgenosed rattlesnakes, are just 1 foot (0.3 meter) long. These tiny rattlesnakes weigh about 4 ounces (113 grams).

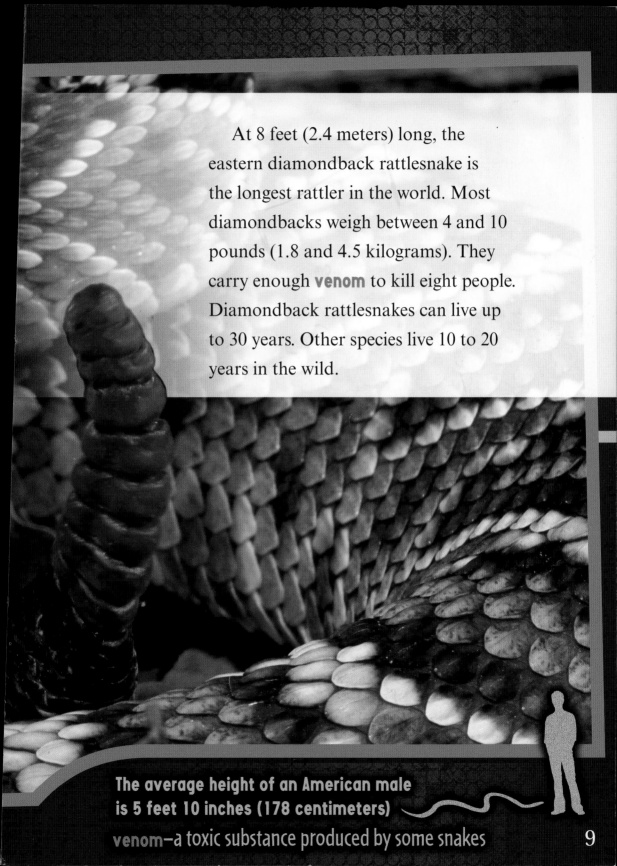

At 8 feet (2.4 meters) long, the eastern diamondback rattlesnake is the longest rattler in the world. Most diamondbacks weigh between 4 and 10 pounds (1.8 and 4.5 kilograms). They carry enough **venom** to kill eight people. Diamondback rattlesnakes can live up to 30 years. Other species live 10 to 20 years in the wild.

The average height of an American male is 5 feet 10 inches (178 centimeters)

venom—a toxic substance produced by some snakes

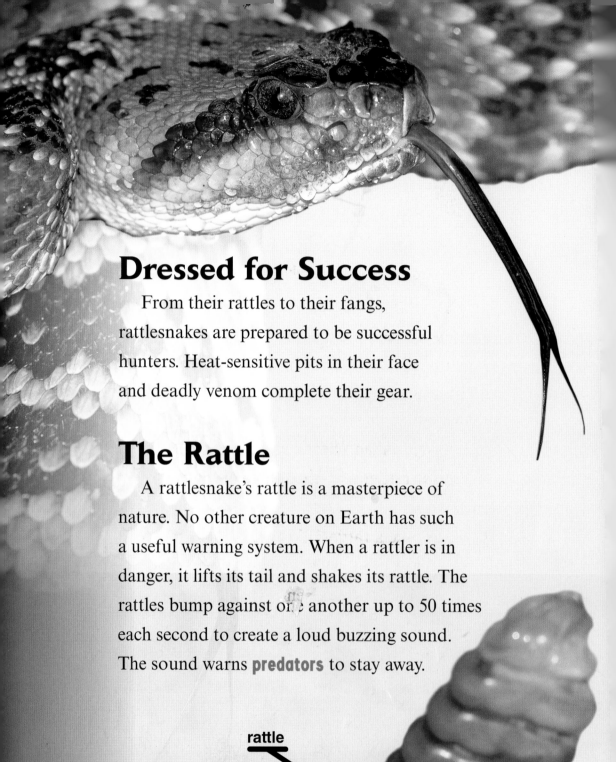

Dressed for Success

From their rattles to their fangs, rattlesnakes are prepared to be successful hunters. Heat-sensitive pits in their face and deadly venom complete their gear.

The Rattle

A rattlesnake's rattle is a masterpiece of nature. No other creature on Earth has such a useful warning system. When a rattler is in danger, it lifts its tail and shakes its rattle. The rattles bump against one another up to 50 times each second to create a loud buzzing sound. The sound warns **predators** to stay away.

rattle

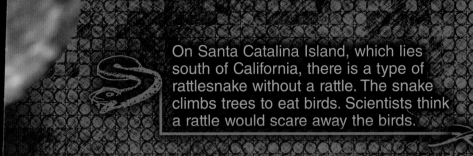

On Santa Catalina Island, which lies south of California, there is a type of rattlesnake without a rattle. The snake climbs trees to eat birds. Scientists think a rattle would scare away the birds.

The rattle is formed when a rattlesnake sheds its scales. A rattlesnake's scales are made of **keratin**, the same material human fingernails are made of. When most snakes shed, all their scales come off. But when a rattler sheds, the thick scale at its tail does not fall off. It sticks to the snake's tail and becomes part of the rattle. A healthy rattler may shed three or four times each year.

Each time a rattlesnake sheds, a new segment is added to its tail. A captive rattlesnake once grew a tail with 38 segments! But most wild rattlesnakes have four to seven segments in their rattles. Sometimes their rattles snag rocks or sticks and break off.

predator–an animal that hunts other animals for food
keratin–the hard substance that forms hair and
fingernails; snake scales are also made of keratin

An American Mascot

In 1754, Benjamin Franklin thought the rattlesnake would be a good symbol for America. He said that the rattler was brave, avoided fighting, and never wounded its enemy without giving fair warning.

During the American Revolution (1775–1783), the rattlesnake was displayed on a bright yellow flag that read, "Don't Tread on Me." This flag is called the Gadsden flag after its designer, Christopher Gadsden.

DONT TREAD ON ME

Heat Seekers

Rattlesnakes belong to a group of snakes called pit vipers. This type of snake can find a tiny mouse in total darkness. Pit vipers find their prey using heat-seeking pits on the sides of their faces. The pits are located between the nose and the eye. Warm prey, like mice, give off heat waves. The waves enter the snake's pits and hit a sensitive pink tissue. This triggers nerves that tell the snake exactly where to strike. Cottonmouths and copperheads are also pit vipers.

heat-seeking pit

13

Taking Care of Business

As a rattler's body uncoils for a strike, its fangs move into position. When the snake's mouth opens, the fang tips fly forward and lock into place. Then the needle-like fangs are ready to deliver the venom.

With fangs longer than those of other snakes, a rattlesnake can sink venom deep into prey. But long fangs can cause problems. To avoid pricking the snake's lower jaws, the fangs fold out of the way when not in use.

Venom Factory

A **gland** on each side of the snake's head makes and stores venom. When a snake bites into an animal, the venom squirts down a tube, through the fangs, and into the prey.

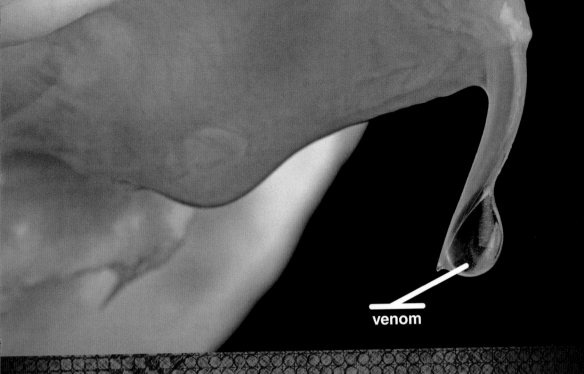

venom

Each type of rattlesnake has a unique blend of deadly chemicals in its venom that works in different ways. When a prairie rattler bites into prey, its venom attacks the prey's blood and organs. The venom tears the cells apart, causing extreme pain. When a Mojave rattlesnake sinks its fangs into prey, the venom stuns the nerves. The prey will not feel much pain, but its organs will soon stop working.

About one-third of rattlesnake bites to humans are "dry." The snake bites without injecting any venom.

gland—an organ that produces chemicals or substances that are used by the body

Sensing Prey

Snakes are known for their long, forked tongues. But these tongues aren't for tasting. Instead, a rattlesnake uses its tongue to pick up nearby smells. As its tongue flicks in and out, it gathers scents in the air and on the ground. When the snake closes its mouth, the tongue brings the collected smells to the roof of its mouth. This area is called the Jacobson's organ. It helps the snake recognize prey.

Rattlesnakes have camouflage coloring that helps them blend in with their surroundings. By blending in, the snakes can hide from predators and prey.

A rattlesnake also relies on its ear bones to sense approaching prey. Though a rattlesnake doesn't have ears and can't hear, its ear bones are still very important. The ear bones rest on the jaw bone, allowing the snake to feel nearby vibrations. The snake follows the vibrations to find prey.

Chapter 3

RATTLESNAKE BEHAVIOR

Some rattlesnakes are born in the middle of deserts. There is no shade or food in sight. All the features the snakes are born with can't keep them alive unless they take action. Fortunately, rattlesnakes have developed behaviors to help them survive in harsh desert environments.

Turn up the Heat

Like all reptiles, rattlesnakes are **cold-blooded**. Their body temperature changes to match their surroundings. They depend on heat from the sun, water, rocks, and ground to warm their bodies. When their bodies get too cold, they can't slither, eat, or strike very fast.

Most rattlesnakes live in warm climates. But getting too warm can be deadly for rattlesnakes because they have no way to cool their bodies. To avoid raising their body temperature too much, rattlers in the desert are **nocturnal**. They only hunt at night. During the day, they rest under rocks or in holes.

cold-blooded–having a body temperature that changes with the surroundings

nocturnal–active at night and resting during the day

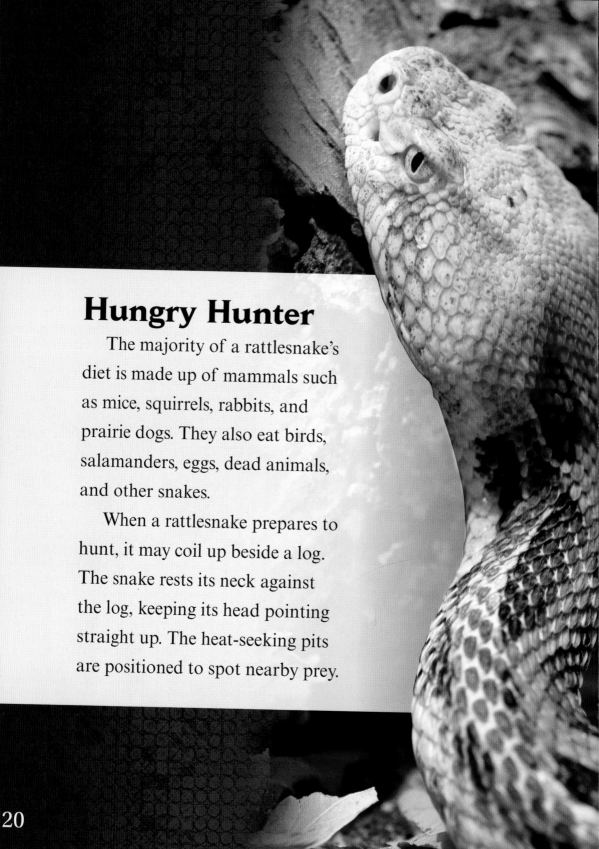

Hungry Hunter

The majority of a rattlesnake's diet is made up of mammals such as mice, squirrels, rabbits, and prairie dogs. They also eat birds, salamanders, eggs, dead animals, and other snakes.

When a rattlesnake prepares to hunt, it may coil up beside a log. The snake rests its neck against the log, keeping its head pointing straight up. The heat-seeking pits are positioned to spot nearby prey.

Soon tiny feet scamper along the log.
A mouse smells danger and freezes. But the
snake has already sensed the mouse's body heat.
The snake strikes and pumps venom into the
prey. The mouse begins to hop away, but the
rattler tracks it. With each flick of its tongue,
the snake smells the air and follows the prey.
When the mouse falls, the snake moves in for
dinner. The stunned mouse can't even put up a fight.

Hibernating

Some rattlesnakes **hibernate** during the winter. The snakes sleep in caves or holes in the ground. Snakes that live in cooler climates may hibernate for up to seven months. Other snakes hibernate for just a few days.

Rattler Roommate

Standing in the desert, Dr. Gordon Schuett stuck a long pole into a dark hole. A video camera taped on the end of the pole showed a diamondback rattler in a pack rat's den. Diamondbacks often eat pack rats and steal their dens. But that's not what happened in this den. Dr. Schuett watched as a pack rat crawled right over the rattler. The snake didn't move!

The diamondback had munched on rats from April through October. But now it was winter, and the hibernating snake wasn't interested in eating its roommate. Dr. Schuett watched the pack rat seal the den with cactus bits, keeping out the cold air. Maybe the two animals were helping each other survive the winter.

Spring Fever

During the mating season in spring, males track down females by smell. If two males are tracking the same female, they compete in a combat dance. They rear up in the air and wrestle. The loser is thrown to the ground. The winner mates with the female.

Unlike most reptiles, rattlesnakes don't lay eggs. The mother holds the young inside her body in clear, thin sacs. About four to 30 babies are born at one time. Baby rattlesnakes look and act like small adults, but they are born without rattles. The rattles form during their second shedding.

Chapter 4

A DANGEROUS WORLD

A rattlesnake's life is full of danger. There are many predators to watch out for. Alligators, badgers, and skunks look for tasty rattlesnake dinners. Red-tailed hawks swoop out of the sky to clamp sharp talons around the snakes. The birds then peck the snakes with razor-like beaks before eating them. Kingsnakes are a serious threat because they are not bothered by rattler venom. Kingsnakes wrap their bodies around rattlesnakes and squeeze until the rattlers can't breathe.

A Speedy Enemy

A roadrunner starts its attack by running circles around the snake. The bird stabs at the rattler's head with its beak. Then it quickly leaps out of reach of the fangs. The roadrunner darts, stabs, and leaps until the snake is stunned. Then it pinches the snake's body with its bill and slams the snake against the ground.

Rattlesnakes have small enemies too. They can get worms in their stomachs or have ticks on their skin. Rattlesnakes can also catch deadly diseases.

The Human Hand

People are a rattlesnake's worst enemy. They kill more rattlesnakes than any predator. Rattlesnakes are sometimes killed for their skins or rattles. Snakes on the road are often run over on purpose. Some people participate in "rattlesnake roundups." They pour gasoline into the dens of hibernating snakes, killing hundreds at a time. People also move into rattlesnakes' habitats and push the snakes out. Some species, such as the eastern diamondback and massasauga, are now **endangered**.

Fortunately, there are people who help rattlesnakes. Scientists study rattlesnake survival. They remove rattlers from cities and release them into the wild. Others work to heal injured snakes. Groups who care about rattlers teach people to treat them with respect.

endangered—at risk of dying out

GLOSSARY

cold-blooded (KOHLD-bluh-duhd)—having a body temperature that changes with the surroundings

endangered (in-DAYN-juhrd)—at risk of dying out

gland (GLAND)—an organ that produces chemicals or substances that are used by the body

hibernate (HYE-bur-nate)—to spend a period of time in a resting state as if in a deep sleep

keratin (KAIR-uh-tin)—the hard substance that forms hair and fingernails; snake scales are also made of keratin

nocturnal (nok-TUR-nuhl)—active at night and resting during the day

predator (PRED-uh-tur)—an animal that hunts other animals for food

reptile (REP-tile)—a cold-blooded animal that breathes air and has a backbone; most reptiles lay eggs and have scaly skin

segment (SEG-ment)—one of many parts

species (SPEE-sheez)—a specific type of animal or plant

talon (TAL-uhn)—a long, sharp claw

venom (VEN-uhm)—a toxic substance produced by some snakes

READ MORE

Lockwood, Sophie. *Rattlesnakes*. World of Reptiles. Chanhassen, Minn.: Child's World, 2006.

Markle Sandra. *Rattlesnakes*. Animal Predators. Minneapolis: Lerner Publications, 2010.

Menon, Sujatha. *Discover Snakes*. Discover Animals. Berkeley Heights, N.J.: Enslow Publishers, 2009.

INTERNET SITES

FactHound offers a safe, fun way to find Internet sites related to this book. All of the sites on FactHound have been researched by our staff.

Here's all you do:

Visit *www.facthound.com*

Type in this code: 9781429654340

INDEX